The Middletown Farm

(The farm in the middle of town)

Acknowledgement

I would like to thank my family for the encouragement and inspiration to finally put a few of my story ideas down in print.
The Middletown Farm series is dedicated to all my children and grandchildren. Their unique perspective on everyday life is a joy and inspiration to me.
The characters in this book are loosely based on things that my children and grandchildren may have said or done.

I hope you enjoy the second book in this series.

Wearing Clothes

By Michael Malenfant

One warm sunny morning Sally Anne was in her backyard singing and twirling and pretending she was flying like a bird in the sky.

As she flew near the barn, she saw
Lady Duck jumping and shaking
wildly.
She was trying to shake off a small
feed sack that somehow got stuck
around her neck.

"Ha, ha, ha," giggled Sally Anne. "You sure look funny wearing that dress."

"What do you mean, Sally Anne?" asked Lady Duck.

"I mean that old bag around your neck looks like you are wearing a pretty little dress."

"I think that it looks very pretty on you," said Sally Anne.
"It does?"
"Ha, ha, yes; you're the best-looking duck on the farm."

And Lady smiled a great ducky smile.

As they were talking, Mrs. Goose strolled out of a small puddle she was enjoying and came over to see what all the laughing was about.

"What are you two talking and laughing about today?" asked Mrs. Goose.

"Hi, Mrs. Goose," said Sally Anne. "I was just admiring Lady's new dress."

"Isn't she pretty?"

"Well I want to wear a dress, too,"
said Mrs. Goose. "Can you find one for me?"

"Here, you can wear mine," said Sally Anne.
So she took off her dress and put it on Mrs. Goose.

"How do I look everyone?"
"You look silly." said Lady Duck.
"No, she doesn't," said Sally Anne. "I think she is the prettiest goose on the farm."

And Mrs. Goose smiled a great goosy smile.

Just then, Peter J. Hogg wandered over to see what all the commotion was about. "What's going on here?" asked Peter.

"Hello Peter," said Sally Anne. "Lady Duck and Mrs. Goose are just learning about wearing clothes. Aren't they both very pretty in their dresses?"
"Hey, I want to wear a dress too!" exclaimed Peter.
"Can you find a dress for me?"

"Silly Peter, boys don't wear dresses."

"But I want to be pretty, too."

"Ha, ha. Boys are supposed to be handsome; only girls are pretty," giggled Sally Anne.
"Here, let me put my hair ribbon around your neck like a tie."

"See, now you are the most handsome pig on the farm."

And Peter smiled a great piggy smile.

Now all of this laughing caught the attention of Penny the hen, who loves a good laugh.

"What's going on over here?" asked Penny.
"Well, we're all playing dress-up today."
"Isn't everyone really pretty?"

Penny could hardly believe her eyes. "Ha, ha, ha, ha," she laughed. "You all look very, very silly!" And then she pooped out several eggs; poop, poop, poop, poop.

"Hey, I want to be pretty, too!" said Penny. "Can you find a dress for me?"
"Well I don't have any more dresses to give you; but in exchange for all these eggs, I will let you wear my socks."
"It's a deal," said Penny.

So Sally Anne took off her shoes and socks.
"Come over here Penny. Let's see if they fit."

As luck would have it, they fit perfectly.
"Do I look pretty wearing my new socks?" Penny asked.

They all laughed and said,
"You have the prettiest hen's feet on the farm."

And Penny smiled a great henny smile.

While they were all admiring how nice they looked, everyone stopped when Sally Anne's mother called out from the house, "Sally Anne, time to come in for lunch."

"Oh no!" cried Sally Anne.
"I need to get all my clothes back right now!"

"No!" yelled all of the animals; and they began to run away in different directions.
"Wait, wait!" yelled Sally Anne as she chased after them.

They were zigzagging everywhere, and Sally Anne almost caught one of them but slipped and fell into the mud puddle.

All the animals stopped running and came back to see if Sally Anne was alright.

As Sally Anne looked up, she could see her mother staring down at her.

Her mother couldn't believe her eyes. There was Sally Anne sitting in a big mud puddle with all the animals wearing her clothes. Sitting nearby was a big pile of eggs.

"Oh no, Sally Anne!" exclaimed her mother. "What on earth happened here? I can't wait to hear you explain this one." What was Sally Anne going to say now?

So Sally Anne told her mother the whole story, right from the beginning, but I doubt that her mother believed any of it.
Do you?

The End